CONTEMPORARY MUSICIANS
AND THEIR MUSIC™

Yellowcard

Amy Breguet

The Rosen Publishing Group, Inc., New York

For Alyssa, my favorite YA

Published in 2007 by The Rosen Publishing Group, Inc.
29 East 21st Street, New York, NY 10010

Copyright © 2007 by The Rosen Publishing Group, Inc.

First Edition

Library of Congress Cataloging-in-Publication Data

Breguet, Amy.
Yellowcard / by Amy Breguet.—1st ed.
   p. cm.—(Contemporary musicians and their music)
Includes bibliographical references (p.   ) and discography (p.   ).
ISBN 1-4042-0714-7 (library binding)
1. Yellowcard (Musical group)—Juvenile literature. 2. Punk rock musicians—United States—Biography—Juvenile literature. I. Title. II. Series.

ML3930.Y45B74 2006
782.42166092'2—dc22

                                                                2005031235

Manufactured in Malaysia

On the cover: The members of Yellowcard, Longineu Parsons III, Ben Harper, Pete Mosely, Ryan Key, and Sean Mackin *(from left)*, greet the paparazzi as they arrive at the 2005 MTV Movie Awards.

Contents

Introduction

Most contemporary song lyrics offer a glimpse into the lives and experiences of the artists behind them. The words in Yellowcard's single "Way Away" are no exception. When Ryan Key sings of breaking out and leaving, he alludes, in part, to what was probably the smartest move the band ever made.

In 2000, Yellowcard's five members left their hometown of Jacksonville, Florida, to try to make California dreamin' a reality. Far from

(From left) Mosely, Key, Mackin, Parsons, and Harper take over the stage at the 2004 Vans Warped Tour in Atlanta, Georgia, demonstrating why their live performances are so popular with their fans.

going "downhill," as the song suggests, things have looked nowhere but up since that leap of faith. Yellowcard is one of the hottest bands on both the punk rock and pop scenes today. With a double-platinum album, an MTV video award, and a spot on the musical festival Warped Tour's main stage under their belt, these twentysomething rockers clearly have something fans want—and keep on demanding.

Along with frontman Ryan Key, age 25, the band's current members include Pete Mosely (bass and vocals), 26; Ryan Mendez (guitar), 25; Longineu Parsons "LP" III (drums), 25; and Sean Mackin (violin and vocals), 26. The band's original guitarist, Ben Harper, 24, left in November 2005 *(see page 38)*. Few young bands can claim use of a classical instrument, an element that fans and critics agree makes Yellowcard stand out. But the band's flair for the fiddle isn't the only thing that sets it apart. For example, there's also its unmatched energy. The band, according to fans, gets the crowd going as few others can—and Warped Tour organizers clearly took notice. After just two stints on the wildly popular tour, Yellowcard was bumped up to the coveted main stage.

Today, Yellowcard is busy with its own world tours as well as promotion of its fifth album. Band members say the personal and musical growth they've experienced since coming together

Ryan Key delivers a passionate performance in Fullerton, California, in 2004. Key, originally from Florida, is a huge fan of another singer/songwriter with southern roots, Ben Folds. Both Key and Folds have intense voices and emotional lyrics.

in 1997 is reflected in their latest tracks. "The songs have lost that adolescent bounciness," Key told a *Rolling Stone* reporter. "They've come into adulthood a bit."

If fans love Yellowcard, the feeling is notably mutual. Even while rising to stardom, Yellowcard continued playing the backyard barbecues, school events, and other venues that gave the band its start. Shows like these, according to the band's Web site, are critical for making a "direct musical connection" with people. There seems no chance for disconnect anytime soon. As one fan summarizes in a posting on the site, "You guys bring everything to the table, originality, great sound, charisma, and soo [*sic*] much more."

Chapter One

"It All Just Clicked"

For the boys who would become Yellowcard, music was never a free-time filler. It was central to their lives. They attended a performing-arts high school together in their hometown of Jacksonville, and some of them were playing music before they could even read. How they came together is an interesting tale of talent blending, good timing, and above all, friendship.

To Each His Own

Although Yellowcard's early members all attended Douglas Anderson School of the Arts, they were each doing their own thing—and none of it seemed to point to the formation of a pop-punk band.

The prestigious Douglas Anderson School of the Arts was established in 1985 in Jacksonville, Florida. The public high school is where the original Yellowcard members first met.

Four of them, Mackin, Harper, Mosely, and Parsons, studied jazz and classical music, but they had different interests even within those subjects. In a 2002 interview with Los Angeles, California, radio show host DJ Rossstar, band members reminisced about an annual school event called Battle of the Bands. Each participated, but in his own capacity. "Ben played with his guitar class," Mackin told Rossstar. "I would play [violin] with the orchestra. LP would play [drums] with the orchestra or jazz band." Key had other aspirations altogether— he wanted to be an actor. Still, singing was a part of that. "He got vocal training through musical theater," Mackin continued.

But the band members were nurturing their individual talents well before high school. Mackin noted in the Rossstar interview that he and Key, good friends since childhood, "always played gigs when we were little." The earliest musical training perhaps belongs to Parsons, the son of renowned jazz trumpet player Longineu Parsons II. Having first sat in front of a drum kit at age two, the junior Parsons was playing professionally by age thirteen, touring the world with his father's band. "Working with my dad broke me into the music world pretty well," Longineu Parsons III told a reporter at *Modern Drummer* magazine. Becoming Yellowcard, however, was something these young musicians did quite on their own.

And So It Begins

As musicians, these high school friends had their own talents, interests, and styles. As for musical tastes, they had at least one in common: punk rock. Hanging out together often meant listening to punk at parties. When original guitarist Harper decided to start a punk band in 1997, Yellowcard was born. This early band included only two of its later members: Harper and Parsons. Classmates Ben Dobson (lead vocals), Warren Cooke (bass), and Todd Clary (guitar and vocals) made up the rest of the band.

In addition to playing in his new band, Harper was regularly jamming with classmate Mackin at local coffeehouses and bookstores. The two friends were writing and playing classical pieces, in line with their training and backgrounds. Then, an innovative idea hit: could violin lend itself to punk music? Wanting to find out, Harper invited Mackin to play a song with his band. Reactions were positive. "Kids thought it was neat and different," Mackin told DJ Rossstar. "I never went away . . . [I] evolved into the band." With that, Yellowcard had eliminated a major risk: the risk of ever being typical.

Finding the "Key"

The late 1990s were marked by journeys of self-discovery for the band. Yellowcard recorded its first and little-known albums, *Midget Tossing* and *Where We Stand*, while solidifying its style

What's a Yellow Card, Anyway?

"Yellow card" is a term used to warn players in soccer. Before ever becoming a band, Yellowcard members would use the soccer term to mean "party foul," according to their Web site. For example, if someone knocked over a drink at a party, witnesses would say, "Yellow card!" (That's no mistake, by the way: while the band name is one word, the soccer term is two.)

and sound. Meanwhile, former classmate Ryan Key had dropped out of Florida State University (where Mackin was also going) after one semester to pursue his dream of making music. He played briefly with the band Modern Amusement before moving to Santa Cruz, California, where he joined another punk band, Craig's Brother. A few months and some artistic differences later, Key decided to return home.

Yellowcard found itself ringing in the new millennium without a lead singer, as Ben Dobson had left the band. Ben Harper invited Key, who was conveniently between projects, to come jam with Yellowcard—and the rest is history. "We started playing songs I had written, and it all just clicked," Key says on the band's Web site. "Sean and I had always been really tight and I had a good relationship with the rest of the guys. It just seemed to work very naturally somehow." Reenergized, Yellowcard was ready to see just what it could do.

We Gotta Get Out of This Place

Key had known since high school graduation what he wanted to do with his life. He was going to make it in the music industry. At last with a band he felt great about, he was more driven than ever.

Yellowcard heats up the stage at the Country Day School of the Sacred Heart in Bryn Mawr, Pennsylvania, in 2004. The band gave a performance at a lucky fan's school as part of a promotion.

Having spent some time on the West Coast already, Key felt strongly that this was where Yellowcard needed to be if its members wanted any chance of real success. "The scene is really, really receptive there," he said in a 2001 interview with punkinterviews.com. "The kids just love new music. The clubs there are just where it's happening. It wasn't to . . . bail on our bands from home or our hometown; it was just [to] kind of expand our horizons and go for it."

He soon persuaded the other band members to leave Jacksonville and head for Southern California. For them, this meant bidding farewell to all things familiar and comfortable, in hopes of finding something more. "It was one of the scariest things of our lives," Mackin told DJ Rossstar of the move to Ventura County in California. "We didn't know that many people." Despite fears and doubts, Yellowcard stayed focused on what they knew best: making great music.

Introducing . . . Yellowcard

To get a break in any business, it helps to know someone. Fortunately, Yellowcard bassist Warren Cooke had an indirect connection to someone at Lobster Records, a progressive label in California. Before moving, the band had sent a demo to Lobster, and producers liked what they heard. Yellowcard released what the guys consider their debut album, *One for the Kids*, on Lobster in 2001. (The band doesn't consider its previously recorded albums, of which only 1,000 copies each were made, to be true representations of Yellowcard.)

With that release, the Yellowcard buzz had quietly but surely begun. Perhaps more important, the band members' own parents—whose reactions had ranged from uncertainty to rage when their sons set off to chase a dream—started to come around. "Something changed when we sent home copies of *One for the Kids,*" Key told a reporter at SoundTheSirens.com. "I think at that point [our parents] understood that we were really serious about making music a way of life."

The following year, Yellowcard released a second album, *The Underdog EP*, on punk-oriented label Fueled by Ramen. Like *One for the Kids*, *Underdog* featured songs that Key had written before joining the band, and it was received just as well. Far from giving the band a sense of complacency, these early successes only drove Yellowcard's members to work harder. They made an effort to take every gig they could, not excluding school events, suburban veterans' halls, living rooms, and backyards. That perseverance, the band would soon find out, would pay off.

Chapter Two

Making It

With the release of two successful albums, Yellowcard—by now comprising the members fans know best (Harper, Key, Mosely, Parsons, and Mackin)—had made a solid start toward industry success. The five friends continued to play live, whether opening for bands they loved or rocking high school cafeterias. By mid-2002, things really started happening for Yellowcard—and fast.

Warped Tour

Around the same time they released *Underdog*, Yellowcard members got an opportunity they'd only dreamed of before. It was the ultimate career boost, something for which young bands every-where annually vie. Yellowcard was invited to join the Warped Tour.

Key answers questions during a backstage interview at the 2004 Vans Warped Tour. Harper *(far right)* scopes the audience.

The Vans Warped Tour is a punk music and extreme sports festival sponsored by skateboarding-shoe manufacturer Vans. Hitting venues across the country every summer since 1995 and internationally since 1998, the massive concert features up-and-coming artists who show unique potential. As tour organizers were forming their lineup for 2002, Yellowcard more than fit that bill.

Technically, it wasn't the first time any of the band members had participated in the Warped Tour. Key, in fact, was a veteran of sorts. "I volunteered to work at Warped Tour every summer it came to Jacksonville, when I was in high school," Key told MTV News in 2004. "I would show up at 6 a.m. and make 50 bucks for the day and be there until three in the morning the next day—working, building ramps and running to get food for people." His gofer days long past, Key, along with his bandmates, was about to experience the festival from where he belonged: the stage.

Yellowcard already had the talent, the energy, and the sound. With the Warped Tour, the young band was now getting the exposure. One more detail—a major label—would seemingly complete the dream. "We . . . basically just played everywhere and anywhere in L.A. and around the country," Key said in a SoundTheSirens interview, "until someone noticed who we were." Someone was about to do just that.

The Way to *Ocean Avenue*

If asked about memorable years, members of Yellowcard would probably cite 1997, the year they came together; 2000, the year they headed to the West Coast; and, most likely, 2003, the year that made them.

Just months after hooking up with Warped Tour, Yellowcard became involved with recording and producing giant Capitol Records, based in Los Angeles. Band members knew then that fans weren't the only ones appreciating their energetic shows. "Our live performance has always been the most important part of the band," Key told SoundTheSirens. "I think the people at Capitol just loved the passion we brought on stage with us, whether we were in front of 5 people or 500." Capitol signed the fivesome, who now shared a label with the likes of the Beastie Boys, Coldplay, Fiona Apple, Snoop Dogg, Kylie Minogue, Jimmy Eat World, and the Red Hot Chili Peppers—and those are just today's artists. One of the oldest major studios, Capitol is also the name behind many timeless recordings of Judy Garland, Frank Sinatra, Nat King Cole, the Beach Boys, and the Beatles. There was no denying it: Yellowcard had joined the big leagues.

In July 2003, Yellowcard released its true breakout album and its first with Capitol, *Ocean Avenue*. Fans devoured the major-label debut, which sold more than half a million copies in a few short months. Featuring the singles "Ocean Avenue," "Way Away," and "Only One," the album proved Yellowcard was one to watch.

As some fans listened to the new CD, those who scored tickets to Warped Tour 2003 got to see Yellowcard do their thing, as the band was on its second stint with the concert at the time of *Ocean*'s release. Ironically, though, the at-home listeners weren't hearing quite the same band as the Warped audience. Pete

Mosely, who had joined the band earlier in the year and played bass on *Ocean Avenue*, took some time off soon after recording the album. Alex Lewis took over bass duties for several gigs, including the Warped Tour. The band, however, would be back to its old self in no time. Mosely returned in 2004.

Riding *Ocean's* Wave

Becoming big adds a critical new word to any star's vocabulary: "publicity." Selling oneself doesn't stop. On the contrary, it becomes serious business. After releasing *Ocean Avenue* and wrapping up Warped Tour 2003, Yellowcard had little time to switch gears before continuing to plug away both on the concert circuit and in the mainstream media. Suddenly, the band was headlining shows, playing internationally, and touring with bands like Matchbook Romance and Less Than Jake. Its singles shot up the Billboard and Top 40 charts, and by the end of 2004, *Ocean Avenue* would be certified double platinum by the Recording Industry Association of America.

For some bands, this whirlwind of newfound fame might mean the end of a personal connection with fans. Yellowcard ensured just the opposite. The band made a point to continue playing at some of its longtime favorite venues—America's high

Pete Mosely, Ben Harper, Ryan Key, Longineu Parsons III, and Sean Mackin *(from left)* pose for the camera in this 2005 photograph. The bandmates cite friendship as an impetus for their success.

schools. The unusual tour stops, which heightened in the months surrounding *Ocean*'s release, happened as often as the band could manage. Yellowcard advertised its affinity for playing free high school gigs on its Web site, where teenage fans were invited to e-mail a request for a private concert. "The cool thing was that we played for a lot of kids that wouldn't have even thought of listening to us," former bassist Alex Lewis told a reporter at *Life in a Bungalo Digest*. "You never knew what kind of school it was. For all we knew, the kid who e-mailed us could have been the only one at the school who knew who we are. Those were the best schools."

Having played their hearts out for nearly a year following the buildup to and smashing success of *Ocean Avenue*, Yellowcard members more than deserved what happened in early 2004. After two years on the Warped Tour's second stage, the band was offered a slot on its prestigious main stage, reserved for nothing

PUNK

Anthony Kiedis of the Red Hot Chili Peppers

Coined in the 1970s, the term "punk rock" refers to a rejection of traditionally popular culture, including its music—such as disco and heavy metal. Punk rock songs tend to be short and simple in structure. They often feature lyrics that make statements about politics and social issues. Blondie and the Ramones are examples of classic punk bands. As the punk sound has become more mainstream, the term "pop punk" is used to describe many popular bands—including Yellowcard and its contemporaries, such as the Red Hot Chili Peppers.

Key, Mosely, and Mackin *(from left)* get the crowd moving at MTV's New York studio in 2004. MTV frequently features up-and-coming bands on its popular afternoon program, *Total Request Live*.

less than budding icons of punk rock. It was "the greatest and most exciting honor," Key told *USA Today* that spring, perhaps not knowing there would be many more to come.

Hitting the Small Screen

As Yellowcard's popularity grew, fans no longer had to take in a concert to get a good look at Key, Mackin, Mosely, Harper, and Parsons. They only had to turn on the TV.

Soon after the band's first single, "Way Away," hit airwaves, the song's accompanying video premiered on Fox's immensely

Key *(left)* and Mackin sing on *The Tonight Show with Jay Leno* in 2004. By the end of 2004, the band had performances on national television and a double-platinum album under its belt.

popular show *The O.C.* Later, the "Ocean Avenue" video became a quick staple on MTV's *Total Request Live.* In April 2004, Yellowcard, along with Solange Knowles, Usher, Ludacris, and others, was featured on TRL's High School Week, when students from across the country ran the show from its Times Square studio in New York.

Then there was the talk-show circuit. Among Yellowcard's early appearances was a guest spot on ABC's *Jimmy Kimmel Live* in November 2003. The late-night gigs continued the following year, as the band performed on *Late Night with Conan O'Brien* and twice on *The Tonight Show with Jay Leno*.

Yellowcard's video work and live performances seemed both to converge and culminate at the 2004 MTV Video Music Awards. At the August 29 event, Yellowcard gave a live performance of "Ocean Avenue" and watched the song's video beat five other hits to win the MTV2 Award. (The video had also been nominated for two other awards: Viewer's Choice and Best New Artist in a Video.) Yellowcard's reaction to the triumph? "Complete chaos and shock," Harper told an interviewer for Canada's ThePunkSite.com. "I don't know how to describe that moment. Ryan was freaking out, he was crying, jumping up . . . like he just won three million dollars or something. It was that kind of emotion." Key's reaction was understandable, considering that his lifelong dream was coming true.

Chapter Three

Inside the Sound

Yellowcard is among today's bands that are difficult to classify. One thing Yellowcard is not, as its Web site states, is "your typical young punk band." Its sound, history, and all else about the band make that perfectly clear. For starters, few of Yellowcard's punk contemporaries feature a classically trained violinist. Also worth factoring in is the musical growth Yellowcard has experienced since coming together in 1997. Labeled punk at the start, and perhaps rightfully so, Yellowcard's music has been described in a variety of ways since then, including emo-core, rock, and pop. To the Jacksonville five, though, all that matters is producing songs they love to play and that their fans love to hear.

Besides playing the violin, Sean Mackin sings in Yellowcard, most notably in the song "Twentythree" on *Ocean Avenue*. Mackin is also known for his stage antics: he often entertains fans by doing backflips during the band's concerts.

Growing from Their Roots

In their youth, the friends who comprise Yellowcard had extensive musical exposure and training. But most of what they learned could hardly apply to punk rock, the genre with which the band is most associated—or could it?

Take Parsons, for example. The son of accomplished musician Longineu Parsons II, he can't remember a time he wasn't immersed in exciting blends of rhythm and sound. Now, Yellowcard reaps the benefit of that solid and unique foundation. "Everything I do is related to the past in some form or fashion," he told *Modern Drummer*. "I grew up playing jazz, and I went on to play a lot of funk and fusion. Yeah, you bet I incorporate a lot of what I learned in the past to what I do now [with Yellowcard]. Definitely."

Then there's Sean Mackin with his trademark violin, taught through the Suzuki method (a common technique of classical teaching). Passionate about his craft yet itching to transcend his training, Mackin started picking up guitar riffs on violin with the early Yellowcard. Before he knew it, he'd become something of a pioneer of violin rock. "When we first started out we got a lot of funny looks," Mackin said in an interview with online magazine *Pop Matters*. "Now it's like, 'You make it cool for us violinists or orchestra nerds to play our music out.'" Even instrument manufacturers, according to *Pop Matters*, are catching on: Yamaha, Zeta, and Jordan have all come out with electric stringed instruments and amps designed for rock. Whether or not Mackin single-handedly launched this apparent new trend, Yellowcard is right at its center. "At some shows, people play air drums or air guitar," Key told MTV News. "Now at our shows, people are playing air violin."

Under the Influences

What else shapes a recording artist's career? Sometimes the answer lies in his or her own CD collection. After all, every artist was once just a fan.

The guys don't deny it. Most of them have been into the punk scene since high school. "I'm a sucker for pop-punk, like Further Seems Forever," Mackin told DJ Rossstar in 2002, going on to name Green Day and Foo Fighters as Key's favorites. Collectively, Mackin said, their favorite band was No Use for a Name, with whom they were touring at the time.

To tour with bands they admire had always been a goal for Yellowcard, even if it meant getting slapped with a label. "We'd

MTV's Vanessa Minnillo chats with Key during a taping of *Total Request Live*. Since MTV's 1981 inception, the network has moved from airing solely music videos to a variety of programs, including this popular music video countdown show.

like to tour with Jimmy Eat World, Green Day, Foo Fighters, Good Charlotte, huge bands . . . it would be so much fun," Mackin told Rossstar. "Just to be lumped in a genre where it could be possible would just be amazing." Joining the Warped Tour, and particularly gracing the main stage, was a huge step in that direction. "I hope this year," Key told MTV News in 2004, "it's a stake that we're putting in the ground that says we've earned the respect of the people at the Warped Tour and the bands we look up to, like NOFX and Bad Religion— bands that have been doing Warped Tour since it started."

Although the band's influences naturally include punk rock, they don't end there. Parsons loves the funk and fusion on which he grew up. He counts Slipknot and Pantera among his favorite metal bands. As evidenced by their chosen paths in school,

Mosely is into jazz, and Mackin, classical. All of these preferences have influenced the band in some way. "Every angle of the spectrum," Mackin said in the Rossstar interview, "brings more into our writing and thought process."

Looking Past Punk

Like many aspiring bands, Yellowcard started out playing what its members liked to listen to and could best emulate. For the bandmates, that meant music falling under the punk and pop-punk genres. Their sound, however, was never some copycat performance. Even from the get-go, it couldn't be, not with the unique talents, training, and backgrounds individual members had. Classical training, in particular, "allows us to expand on a style of music that's sometimes pigeonholed as three-chord rock 'n' roll that all sounds the same," Key told *USA Today*. "We can manipulate a lot of standard chord progressions and turn them into something cooler."

Yellowcard members themselves aren't the only ones who see beyond the band's usual labels. As one article in the Vancouver, Canada, weekly newspaper the *Georgia Straight* reads, "It's difficult to think of Yellowcard simply as a punk band. The vocals dominate, the chugging guitars are crisp and clear, and the choruses make for fist-pumping sing-alongs. And the lyrics are packed with sentiments that wouldn't seem out of place in a personal diary." That lyrical side is likely what has led to the band's recent association with another genre: emo. Evolving from an underground musical movement that started in the 1980s in Washington, D.C., today's emo scene is somewhat broad and difficult to define. One unchanging criterion for emo—short for "emotional hardcore"—is personal, emotional lyrics. That considered, Yellowcard's perceived emo streak isn't exactly a wonder.

A Way with Words

When Key writes lyrics for Yellowcard's tracks, he isn't just giving himself something to sing. Nearly every song tells of something band members feel, believe, or—if you listen hard enough—have been through.

Ocean Avenue is essentially a treasure trove of Yellowcard experiences and philosophies. "Miles Apart" reflects on periods when the friends were leading somewhat separate lives. "Way Away," referenced in the introduction of this book, is about doing what's necessary to find fulfillment. Then, as exciting as that brave journey may be, there's always that subtle longing to be "Back Home"—a sentiment the band expresses in *Ocean*'s final song.

"Only One" is perhaps where Key gets the most personal, singing of a recent and somewhat confusing split with his girlfriend. "It was a weird breakup," he told MTV News. "It was one of those things where I felt like I had to do it, even though she didn't do anything wrong. I just needed some space to figure life out for a while on my own."

Like the rest of the country, Yellowcard members were hit hard by the events of 9/11. But they also gained a new respect for firefighters and others for whom lifesaving is an everyday responsibility. The song "Believe" is evidence of that. "View from Heaven" is another sort of memorial, written for friend and Inspection 12 drummer Scott Shad, who was killed in a car accident at age eighteen.

Through exhilaration and sadness, adventure and tragedy, Yellowcard has lived enough already to write a lifetime's worth of songs. Much more inspiration, however, is likely yet to come.

Chapter Four

Beyond Ocean, New Waters

Think Yellowcard, think *Ocean Avenue*. At least, that's pretty much how it's been until now. On the horizon, though, are several new things with which to associate this nonstop group, starting with a fourth album. And if the band started shedding labels before, its latest projects are sure to finish the job.

New York State of Mind

Two years and counting is a long time for hungry fans to go without a new release. That agonizing spell ended for Yellowcard buffs in January 2006, when the band introduced *Lights and Sounds*. The latest creation, according to a more-than-satisfied Yellowcard, was well worth the wait—not to mention the work.

Parsons, Harper, Mosely, Key, and Mackin *(from left)* enjoy the red-carpet treatment at the 2005 MTV Movie Awards.

In December 2004, Key and Mosely moved to New York City to begin working once again with Neal Avron, the Capitol Records producer behind *Ocean*. Getting started on the project, however, was no simple task. Although the two allowed themselves some much-needed relaxation time upon arriving in the Big Apple, any procrastination was really about something more. "It took us so long to get around to writing because we were scared to death," Mosely admitted to a reporter at MTV.com. "It was the first time we had to write a record for somebody. Every other record we did for ourselves, and we did it on our own terms. We did something that attracted attention to us, and now we have to do something to follow that up and go beyond."

Once the process began, though, the ideas seemed to fly. Key and Mosely remained mainly on the East Coast through the winter, pooling their creativity and taking in sights they'd rarely seen before—like snow. As springtime rolled around, they joined the rest of the band back in Los Angeles to start bringing to life the new songs they had penned. Although the preproduction phase often meant being in a studio from dawn until dusk, Yellowcard was used to such intensity. "We've definitely worked hard on [the album]," Key told MTV.com. "But it was almost like a break compared to the past four years of touring and making *Ocean Avenue.*" As the band recorded nineteen tracks, Yellowcard's next masterpiece finally took form.

Following Holly

So can Yellowcard fans expect more of the sounds they love from the upcoming release? The short answer might be yes and no. Same talented musicians? Check. Expressive lyrics? Check. Violin? Affirmative and then some—a few songs, according to a blog entry by Mosely, feature a full orchestra. But the list of constants just may end there.

Basically, Yellowcard members say, the band has grown up. Still on the edge of adolescence when they wrote and recorded the tracks for *Ocean Avenue*, the friends gradually entered adulthood while rising to the top. Both their personal maturation and growth as a band are reflected on their latest album, which the guys say is far more rock than pop punk. "We were still young musicians on the last one, and it was a bit tentative," Key told MTV.com. "But now our minds are much broader in scope, and we've had more time and freedom to express ourselves. We also had time to clear our heads."

Although adamant that *Lights and Sounds* is not a "concept album," the band explains that the songs are loosely tied together by a story of sorts. A girl named Holly—as in Holly Wood—is lost in Los Angeles. Listeners get to know the symbolic character through songs like "Holly Wood Died" and "Rough Landing Holly." "At times you love her," Key said in the MTV.com interview, "and at times you hate her. At times she's good to you and sometimes she's bad." The album's clear and metaphorical theme, according to MTV, is disdain for Los Angeles as a place to live.

Never exactly a secret—the band contributed to 2004's *Rock Against Bush, Volume 2*—Yellowcard's political ideas

BYE-BYE, BEN; WELCOME ABOARD, RYAN

Ben Harper

Ryan Mendez

In November 2005, Yellowcard confirmed what many fans had long assumed: Ben Harper, Yellowcard's longtime guitarist, had left. While details are scarce, Harper's commitment to Takeover Records, his indie label, seems to be the main issue.

According to a press release, Harper explained: "Due to some ongoing tensions within the band, and some great new opportunities with Takeover bands which have recently presented themselves, it seemed time to take my experiences with Yellowcard and apply them to the development of other new artists and new music-centric media projects."

Before the announcement of Harper's departure, Ryan Mendez (formerly of the band Staring Back) apparently had already replaced him on the band's fall tour. For their part, the bandmates Harper's known since childhood seem to be taking things in stride. "This change is hard for all of us," Pete Mosely said in the release, "but Ben will always be our brother."

come across louder than ever on the band's latest songs. "Two Weeks from Twenty" is a prime example of that. "It's this jazz-lounge anti-war song," Key told a reporter at *Rolling Stone*. "You're listening to this super-smooth, jazzy groove, but we're talking about something that means a lot to us—and that's really cool. It's more intense subject matter than we've ever tried to tackle." Other songs, especially the album's title track, are pure rock—something of which the band is particularly proud. "It's got such an amazing, driving, rock-n-roll vibe to it, with none of that frickin' pop-punk stigma," Key said of the single "Lights and Sounds." "It's . . . something we've been striving to write for a long time, so when we were done, it was a relief: 'We wrote a great rock song!'"

And the Winner Is . . .

With its next album written, recorded, and ready to go, Yellowcard has turned its attention to some other projects. Through these, one thing has become clear: this band can't resist a good contest.

Never ones to rest, Yellowcard members visited America's northern neighbor for its thirteen-date Wish We Were Canadian Tour in September 2005. Fans who came to the scheduled club venues experienced a preview of the band's new album, and one lucky attendee per show got much more: the opportunity to hang out with, interview, and take pictures of the band. That would be the grand prize winner of the Special Correspondent contest, which Yellowcard held in each participating city. In addition to the grand prize winner, four runners-up at each Canadian show got to attend a sound check and meet the band. Following the tour, Yellowcard headed back to the United States for a string of club shows.

"We Rocked as Hard as We Could"

From Jacksonville to Los Angeles, coffee houses to awards shows, and soccer glossaries to music headlines, Yellowcard has few—if any—regrets. On the contrary, the five childhood friends know they succeeded largely because, simply put, they went for it. "I hope we can look back and know that we did exactly what WE wanted to do with our lives. We followed our dreams all the way through," Key told SoundTheSirens. "I want to look back and know we rocked as hard as we could and never gave up."

Timeline

Mid-1990s Future Yellowcard members attend Douglas Anderson School of the Arts together.

1997 Ben Harper forms the first version of Yellowcard.

2000 Ryan Key replaces Yellowcard lead singer Ben Dobson. Yellowcard moves to Southern California.

2001 Yellowcard releases its debut album, *One for the Kids*, on Lobster Records.

2002 Yellowcard releases its follow-up album, *The Underdog EP*, and joins the Vans Warped Tour.

2003 Capitol Records signs Yellowcard, and in July, the band releases its major-label debut, *Ocean Avenue*.

2004 *Ocean Avenue* is certified double platinum. Yellowcard is given a slot on the Warped Tour's main stage.

August 2004 Yellowcard performs its single "Ocean Avenue" at the MTV Video Music Awards. The video wins the MTV2 Award.

Spring/summer 2005 Yellowcard records its next album.

September 2005 Yellowcard embarks on its Canadian tour.

November 2005 Ben Harper leaves the band, and Ryan Mendez replaces him as lead guitarist.

January 2006 *Lights and Sounds* is released.

Discography

Midget Tossing (Takeover Records, 1997, out of print)

Where We Stand (Takeover Records, 1999, rereleased 2004 and 2005)

Still Standing EP (DIY Records, 2000, out of print)

One for the Kids (Lobster Records, 2001)

The Underdog EP (Fueled by Ramen Records, 2002)

Ocean Avenue (Capitol Records, July 2003)

Beyond Ocean Avenue: Live at the Electric Factory (DVD, 2004)

Lights and Sounds (Capitol Records, January 2006)

Glossary

affinity Preference; liking.

allude To make indirect reference.

aspirations Hopes; dreams.

contemporary Current; modern. Someone living at the same time as someone else.

coveted Desired with envy.

culminate To reach the highest point.

debut First; introductory. A first or introductory creative work.

genre Category; classification.

perseverance Persistence; not giving up.

prestigious Reserved for a select few; honorable.

transcend To go beyond.

venue Location where an event takes place.

For More Information

Capitol Records
1750 N. Vine Street
Los Angeles, CA 90028-5209
(323) 462-6252
Web site: http://www.
    capitolrecords.com

Takeover Records
1810 14th Street
Suite 210
Santa Monica, CA 90404
Web site: http://www.
    takeoverrock.com

Web Sites

Due to the changing nature of Internet links, the Rosen Publishing Group, Inc., has developed an online list of Web sites related to the subject of this book. This site is updated regularly. Please use this link to access the list:

http://www.rosenlinks.com/
    cmtm/yell

For Further Reading

Blink-182, with Anne Hoppus. *Blink-182: Tales from Beneath Your Mom*. New York, NY: Pocket Books, 2001.

Bogdanov, Vladimir, Chris Woodstra, and Stephen Thomas Erlewine, eds. *All Music Guide to Rock: The Definitive Guide to Rock, Pop, and Soul*. San Francisco, CA: Backbeat Books, 2002.

George-Warren, Holly, and Patricia Romanowski, eds. *The Rolling Stone Encyclopedia of Rock and Roll*. New York, NY: Fireside, 2001.

Hermes, Will, and Sia Michel, eds. *Spin: 20 Years of Alternative Music; Original Writing on Rock, Hip-Hop, Techno, and Beyond*. New York, NY: Three Rivers Press, 2005.

Myers, Ben. *Green Day: American Idiots and the New Punk Explosion*. Eastbourne, England: Gardners Books, 2005.

Shirley, David. *The History of Rock and Roll*. New York, NY: Franklin Watts, 1997.

Bibliography

Conner, Shawn. "Yellowcard Feels the Pain." *Georgia Straight*,
    July 8, 2004. Retrieved August 25, 2005 (http://www.
    straight.com/content.cfm?id=3759).

D'Angelo, Joe. "Warped Tour Main Stage Is a Long Time
    Coming for Yellowcard." MTV Networks, May 7, 2004.
    Retrieved August 3, 2005 (http://www.vh1.com/artists/
    news/1486886/05072004/yellowcard.jhtml).

Devenish, Colin. "Yellowcard Green No More." *Rolling Stone*,
    June 24, 2005. Retrieved August 3, 2005 (http://www.
    rollingstone.com/news/story/_/id/7420236/yellowcard?
    pageid=rs.Artistcage&pageregion=triple3).

Gorman, Bobby. "Interviews: Yellowcard." October 23, 2004.
    Retrieved August 17, 2005 (http://www.thepunksite.com/
    interviews.php?page=yellowcard2).

Gundersen, Edna. "Yellowcard's 'Ocean' CD Goes Swimmingly."
    USA Today.com, May 3, 2004. Retrieved August 16, 2005
    (http://www.usatoday.com/life/music/news/2004-05-03-
    yellowcard-verge_x.htm).

Koroneos, George. "An Interview with Yellowcard." *Life in a
    Bungalo Digest*, 2004. Retrieved August 18, 2005 (http://
    lifeinabungalo.com/interviews/yellowcard/Yellowcard.htm).

"Longineu Parsons: Punk Passion, Jazz Precision." *Modern Drummer*, December 2005.

Montgomery, James. "Don't You Forget About Yellowcard: Band to Return This Fall." MTV Networks, June 14, 2005. Retrieved August 3, 2005 (http://www.mtv.com/news/articles/1504125/06142005/yellowcard.jhtml).

Montgomery, James. "Yellowcard Move to New York, Write LP About Hating Los Angeles." MTV Networks, August 9, 2005. Retrieved August 16, 2005 (http://www.vh1.com/artists/news/1507272/08092005/yellowcard.jhtml).

Punkinterviews.com. "Yellowcard." Retrieved August 30, 2005 (http://www.angelfire.com/punk2/punkskaemo/page13.html).

Rossstar, DJ. "DJ Rossstar w/ Yellowcard." November 25, 2002. Retrieved August 3, 2005 (http://www.djrossstar.com/yellowcardinterview.html).

Walter, David. "Yellowcard Break from the Mold." SoundTheSirens.com, June 2003. Retrieved August 3, 2005 (http://www.soundthesirens.com/articles/index.php?id=8,79,0,0,1,0).

Yellowcard official Web site. http://www.yellowcardrock.com.

Zemler, Emily. "Strung Out." *Pop Matters*, April 11, 2005. Retrieved August 23, 2005 (http://www.popmatters.com/music/features/050411-cello.shtml).

Index

About the Author

Amy Breguet is a writer working mainly in the field of educational publishing. She lives in Southampton, Massachusetts, with her husband, Charlie, and children, Hope and Casey, ages four and two. She has dabbled in musical theater, admits to a brief karaoke addiction, and enjoys many kinds of popular music. She now counts herself among Yellowcard's fans.

Photo Credits

Cover, pp. 1, 7, 22, 23, 24, 30, 38 (bottom) © Getty Images; pp. 4–5, 17, 21, 38 (top) © Retna Ltd.; p. 9 Courtesy of Douglas Anderson School of the Arts; pp. 13, 27 © Rahav Segev/Retna.com, Retna Ltd.; p. 35 © Lisa O'Conner/Zuma/Corbis.

Designer: Gene Mollica; **Editor:** Jun Lim
Photo Researcher: Gene Mollica